Medieval Weapons and Warfare

Armies and Combat in Medieval Times

Paul Hilliam

The Rosen Publishing Group, Inc., New York

To my family

Published in 2004 by The Rosen Publishing Group, Inc.
29 East 21st Street, New York, NY 10010

First Edition

Library of Congress Cataloging-in-Publication Data

Hilliam, Paul.
Medieval weapons and warfare: armies and combat in medieval times/Paul Hilliam.
    p. cm.—(The library of the Middle Ages)
Summary: A discussion of the tactics and technology of warfare during the Middle Ages, including the tradition of personal combat, the use of armor, castles-and-siege weapons, and the dominance of the mounted knight.
Includes bibliographical references and index.
ISBN 0-8239-3995-2 (library binding)
1. Military art and science—Europe—History—To 1500—Juvenile literature. 2. Middle Ages—Juvenile literature. [1. Military art and science—Europe—History—To 1500. 2. Middle Ages.]
I. Title. II. Series.
U37.H533 2003
355'.0094'0902—dc21

2002151332

Manufactured in the United States of America

Table of Contents

King Henry V of England crosses the Somme River to attack French forces just before the Battle of Agincourt in 1415, from a fifteenth-century French manuscript illumination.

Knights During the Middle Ages

nights in armor, soldiers clashing on the battlefield, and castles under siege are images that excite the imagination. The period of the Middle Ages, between about the years AD 1000 and 1500, may appear on the surface to be one of chivalry and romance, but the reality of war touched everyone, whether noble or common folk, bringing horror and devastation.

Today you can piece together the past by visiting museums, battlefields, and castles. Statues of knights on tombs in churches and cathedrals help to show us what they wore, and written accounts, paintings, and tapestries from the period tell us more about their lives and deeds.

Becoming a Knight

During the early Middle Ages, the term "knight" simply referred to a soldier who went into battle on horseback. As the art of warfare in medieval Europe developed, only the rich could afford to equip themselves with the latest weapons, armor, and suitable horses. Accordingly, knights almost always came from aristocratic and noble families.

Sir Geoffrey Luttrell, an English knight, with two female admirers, from the fourteenth-century Luttrell Psalter, a book of psalms

Preparing to become a knight took many years of training. At the age of about seven, a boy from a noble family would be sent to live at the home of a relative or a neighboring knight. There he served as a page, waiting upon his master at the table and carrying out errands. In return, he was taught the first steps of fighting, using blunt wooden swords. He also learned to wrestle and ride a horse. Later he might practice jousting by charging at a quintain, which was a target at one end of an arm, mounted on a revolving post. If he was too slow, a weighted bag at the other end of the arm would swing around and knock him off his horse!

A knight undergoing religious purification before setting out on a quest, or a military campaign, from a fifteenth-century manuscript illumination

At the age of fourteen, a page was sent to another home or castle where he became a squire. The word "squire" comes from the French word *ecuyer*, meaning "shield-bearer." It was now his job to help a knight put on his armor before battle, and he would also assist a knight if he was injured or unhorsed. Squires were expected to be very fit. They spent long hours developing their sword and jousting skills. It was also important to learn the rules of chivalry, a code that defined how a knight was to behave in times of war and also at court during times of peace. The word "chivalry" is derived from the French word *chevalier*, meaning "horseman."

At the age of about twenty-one, a squire was ready to become a knight, but first it was usual to undergo a ceremony of purification. Often this involved a bath to wash away sins, which was followed by putting on colored robes to symbolize his new position—white for purity, red to show he was prepared to shed his blood for a just cause, and black to show that he was prepared to die. He then spent a night kneeling before the altar in church. The following morning his sword was blessed and he took a vow "to fear God, serve the king, protect the weak, and live honorably." In full armor he then knelt in front of the king, who dubbed (or touched) the knight on the shoulder with the flat side of his sword.

The Feudal System

In 1066, Duke William of Normandy, an area in northern France, conquered England at the Battle of Hastings. The story of the invasion is depicted on a tapestry, which can still be seen in Bayeux, a small town in northern France. William rewarded the nobles who fought for him by giving them land. In return for these gifts of land, William demanded to be paid homage and to be given military service. This became known as the feudal system, from the Latin word *feudum*, meaning "land held." Each noble knelt before William, who was now king, and said: "I promise to become your man, to hold these lands faithfully and perform my due service." The king told his nobles they must always be ready to fight for him, and he also told them how many knights they were expected to bring with them. Bishops were also granted land, and they, too, were expected to provide a certain number of knights when required. William was determined to keep a strong hold on the country he had conquered.

The number of knights each duke, baron, or bishop was expected to provide varied according to the amount of land he governed. The Normans anticipated resistance from the Englishmen they had subdued, and so a program of castle building was quickly undertaken. At first, these castles were made of wood, consisting of a stockade on a mound of earth. Gradually, these were replaced by impressive stone castles, which gave considerable protection for the occupants.

In this fifteenth-century Italian manuscript, a knight pays homage to his lord.

Nevertheless, it was not long before William called upon his nobles for military support when faced by rebellion in the north of England during 1069.

Some nobles housed the knights they commanded in the castles they built. Other nobles granted knights their own estates of land, called manors. These knights were expected to swear homage to their local lord. However, William made sure all knights first swore allegiance to himself as king. He did not want to face rebellion from his lesser vassals. In each village, the peasants were expected to serve the knight who was their local lord. In times of war, this might mean going into battle carrying whatever makeshift weapons were available, if only a farm pitchfork.

Tournaments

It took many years of training to become a knight, so it was important in times of peace to maintain the skills that had been acquired. Tournaments originated in northern France between about 1050 and 1070 and were an excellent way for a knight to prove he was fit for war.

Two types of events developed. The first was a mock free-for-all battle called a mêlée. This was sometimes held between knights from nearby castles, with the aim that one set of knights should capture and hold as many opposing knights as possible. Later, the winning side would ransom the knights it held. Watching knights fight in single combat soon became popular, and stands were specially constructed for the spectators.

In the later Middle Ages, jousting was probably the most spectacular event at a tournament. Jousting involved pairs of

Two knights jousting, from a fourteenth-century manuscript. Jousting was a way to train for real combat.

knights on horseback charging at each other with lances, which were usually blunted with crown-shaped ends called coronals. Knocking another knight off his horse became more difficult as higher-backed saddles were designed. Although a barrier separated horses so that head-on collisions were avoided, the force with which the lances struck and splintered often caused injury and sometimes death, despite the full body armor knights wore in later years.

At the height of their popularity in the thirteenth century, tournaments became as much a spectacle as they were a serious part of a knight's training. Tournaments were held over several days, and there were valuable prizes to be won, such as a new suit of armor or a warhorse. Each day heralds announced who would be participating, identifying each knight by the symbols on his shield and surcoat. The top of a knight's helmet might feature a symbol from a coat of arms, such as a colorful animal.

Entertainment was provided in the evenings. Important guests would banquet and dance at the castle, providing the chance for romance between contestants and noble ladies. The next day, a knight might be granted the favor of a lady by wearing her scarf on his sleeve. This was also the age of courtly love!

Orders of Knights

During the eleventh and twelfth centuries, several groups of military monks were founded. There were three main orders, as they were called: the Knights of St. John, the Knights Templar, and the Knights of the Teutonic Order. The knights who joined these orders took religious vows, promising to be poor, obedient, and chaste (meaning having no sexual relations with women). However, they also promised to use their military skills in holy wars and to protect fellow Christians.

This was the time of the Crusades. Muslim Saracens from the Middle East had captured Jerusalem and the area regarded by Christians in Europe as the Holy Land. In 1095, Pope Urban II called upon the kings and princes of Christian Europe to recapture Jerusalem. The word "crusade" comes from the Latin *crux*, meaning a cross, because the pope told warriors to sew a cloth cross onto their tunics as they went to war.

The Knights of St. John, founded in 1099 when the Christians captured Jerusalem, were also known as the

A manuscript illustration showing the Knights of the Order of the Star paying homage to their lord and banqueting. Such orders were groups of knights who took religious vows to fight for a particular cause. They were very prominent during the Crusades.

Hospitallers because they kept a hospital in Jerusalem where they looked after the sick. The Knights Templar, also founded in 1099, took their name from their headquarters on the Temple Mount in Jerusalem, where they swore allegiance to the patriarch of Jerusalem. The order grew rapidly in number and became very wealthy as admirers donated land in Europe to the knights in an effort to support their work. The Knights of the Teutonic Order originated in Germany and were founded in about 1190. They were also active in eastern Europe, where they helped to spread Christianity to areas in Poland, in Hungary, and near the Baltic Sea.

The knights in these orders devoted their lives to the defense of the Holy Land, particularly in the years between the Crusades. They built huge castles from which they rode out to protect pilgrims. When the Crusades came to an end, the orders spread to other areas of Europe, including Spain, where they fought against the Moors from North Africa, who occupied Spain until 1492.

A full set of armor for a knight and his horse, from Germany, around 1500. The expense of such armor, as well as the expense of maintaining warhorses, ensured that only nobles could afford to equip themselves in this way.

Weapons and Armor

The sword is the weapon most associated with the medieval knight. However, the history of the sword can be traced back 3,000 years. Early swords were made of bronze, which made them rather soft. Later, iron was used, which was harder but relatively brittle, and so swords would often snap in battle. By the Middle Ages, a technique known as pattern-welding had been developed. This involved layering hard and soft iron rods alternately and then twisting and hammering them together. Harder rods were then hammer-welded onto the sword to provide the cutting edges. The metal was then heated in a furnace, plunged into cold water, reheated, and allowed to cool naturally. Finally, the sword was shaped and sharpened.

Because it took so long to make a sword, they were expensive. Good swords were regarded as prize possessions by those who could afford them, principally knights. The best swords were passed on from one generation to the next. The Vikings from Scandinavia gave their swords names, such as Hvati (keen) or Langhrass (long and sharp), and this tradition carried on into the Middle Ages.

Everyone knows that the sword of the legendary King Arthur was called Excalibur.

Between the handle and the blade, a sword had a quillion. This was usually a simple straight bar at right angles to the blade, providing protection to the hand. At the other end of the handle was a pommel, to help prevent loss of grip. The period when a sword was designed can be determined partly by the shape of the pommel, which was D-shaped at the start of the Middle Ages. Later, it was shaped like a Brazil nut, and later still, it became disc-shaped and was often mounted with a coat of arms. If a sword was used more for ceremony, its pommel might be inlaid with a precious stone and it was sheathed in a highly decorated metal scabbard. However, scabbards were usually made of leather and hung from a waist belt called a bawdrick.

The length and shape of swords changed during the Middle Ages. When chain mail was worn as the main form of protective armor, a typical sword was about three feet long and double-edged, with a fairly steep point. It could then be used for both slashing

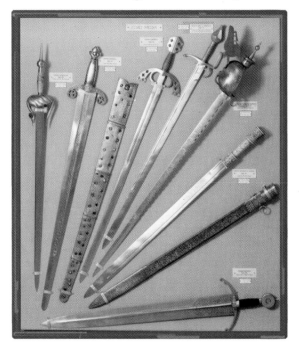

A display of Spanish swords made between the twelfth and fifteenth centuries. As full plate armor replaced chain mail, and it became less important to carry a shield, both hands became free to carry a longer and heavier sword.

and stabbing. As plate armor developed, it was less effective to slash at an opponent, and so knights tried to thrust through chinks and weak spots between various pieces of armor. As a result, swords were made with a sharper, sloping point. Wearing plate armor also meant that knights relied less on protecting themselves by carrying a shield. With two hands free, swords increased in length to between four and five feet, sometimes with a fuller, or shallow groove, along the length of the blade, to help reduce the overall weight. Knights would use these massive swords to deliver crushing blows in an attempt to cause injury and to knock each other over. A short dagger, called a misericord, meaning "dagger of mercy," would also be carried, so a fallen foe might be dispatched quickly.

Other Weapons

In the early Middle Ages, knights on horseback charged at their enemies with a lance, which varied little from the spears used by ordinary foot soldiers. It was the use of a stirrup for the feet, an invention from the Far East, that allowed a knight to control his horse and balance himself on impact. Over the years, knights wore more extensive armor, and so bigger and stronger horses were used. In turn, this meant that much longer and heavier lances could be carried. They were now made from tree trunks, turned on a lathe, and made thicker. Sometimes armor featured a bracket on which to rest the lance for additional support.

After the impact of a charge, knights might continue to fight on horseback, at which point a ball and chain, a war hammer, an axe, or a mace might by used in preference to a sword. The ball and chain featured an iron ball covered in

The heads of two lances, from the sixteenth century. A line of determined foot soldiers with long lances might even foil a cavalry charge.

spikes, which was attached to a short shaft by a chain that was swung at arm's length to give the ball extra force on impact. More common was the war hammer. This had a fairly short shaft with a sharp spike on one side of the head that could pierce through plate armor. On the other side of the head there was a hammer used to dent armor so as to restrict movement. Axes varied in design. In the early Middle Ages, they were huge, with long handles. A Danish or Saxon warrior swinging a large axe could easily knock off a man's head with one blow. Later, smaller axes with shorter shafts were used. The mace was a metal club with an enlarged or flanged head capable of delivering a powerful blow that could cause injury or concussion. Bishop Odo, half brother of William I of England, is shown on the Bayeux Tapestry waving a mace above his head. A bishop or priest was not allowed to spill blood with a sword, but battering one's enemies with a mace was obviously thought to be acceptable.

Armor

During the eleventh and twelfth centuries, knights wore chain mail made from rings of iron that were interlocked to form a shirt called a hauberk or byrnie. The armor came down as far as the knees, at which point it was split to make riding a horse easier. Underneath, a padded garment called an aketon helped to soften sword blows. Over time, the hauberk was extended to include iron sleeves, mittens, and a hood. Helmets were conical in shape and often had a wide nose guard at the front. The weight of all this chain mail was considerable. Knights also carried large, kite-shaped shields made of wood and covered with leather. These shields were slightly curved toward the body, were decorated on the front, and had carrying straps on the back.

By the start of the thirteenth century, the great helm had been introduced to give a knight's face and head extra protection. This was a flat-topped, round-sided, metal box with narrow eye slits at the front. It was very heavy, so it was made long enough to rest on the shoulders, which helped bear its weight. Because the face was now completely covered, knights on the battlefield recognized each other by their coats of arms, painted on their shields and surcoats.

Plate armor started to appear in the fourteenth century. Knights had already experimented with body armor called *cuir bouilli*, which was made from leather. The leather was first boiled and then hardened into shape. Sometimes the leather was reinforced with small metal plates stitched into place. One piece covering the chest could be buckled to another on the back. However, plate armor was regarded as a better defense than leather against the increasing use of arrows in war. Single pieces of armor were shaped individually and strapped over chain mail, at first covering just the legs and arms.

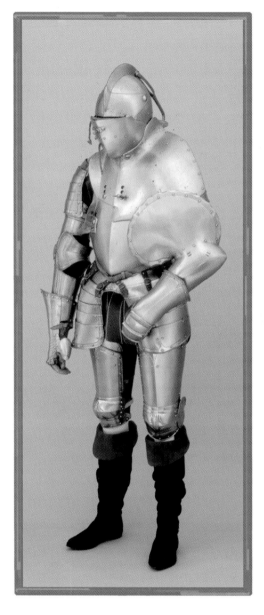

A suit of full body armor, from Saxony, Germany, around 1590. A bracket connects the helmet to the back plate to prevent the helmet from being forced back when struck. The plate covering the left arm has been extended to form a kind of shield.

As the techniques used to fashion armor developed, the helm was replaced by the bascinet, which was a more closely fitted helmet with rounded surfaces to deflect blows. A removable or hinged visor was fitted to make breathing easier, and padding was riveted inside for additional comfort. Chain-mail neck guards called aventails were attached to the bottom of the bascinet with threads. Gauntlets for the hands and sabatons for the feet were made with overlapping plates, and armor was constructed for the shoulders, elbows, and knees to allow for as much natural movement as possible. With such increased protection, the large, kite-shaped shields used earlier by the Normans were replaced by smaller, triangular shields, which were lighter but still slightly curved to hug the body. At the same time, the long

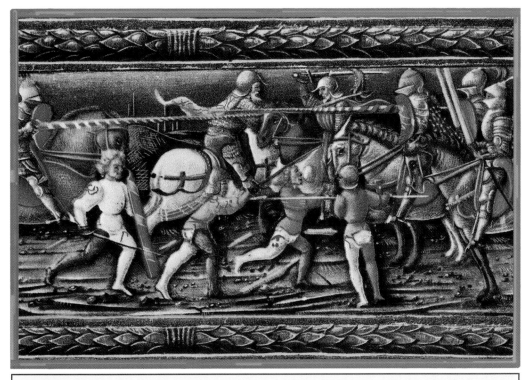

A tournament scene from a fifteenth-century Italian edition of the Bible. A group of knights are jousting and engaging in a mêlée, a free-for-all combat involving more than two combatants.

surcoat was replaced by a shorter jupon, which still showed the coat of arms.

A knight's warhorse was both extremely important and expensive. It was fitted with a cloth covering that bore the knight's coat of arms, but underneath, there was a layer of padding. In the later Middle Ages, armor was made especially for horses. At the very least, a horse would wear a shaffron to cover its head and nose, but sometimes more extensive armor would also cover its neck and sides.

The early fifteenth century found many important centers for the production of complete suits of armor, including Augsburg, Nuremberg, and Passau in Germany; Milan in

Italy; Paris in France; and Greenwich in England. Iron ore was needed, together with coal or charcoal, and some armorers also used waterpower to work heavy hammers and other simple machines. The ways in which different craftsmen worked were jealously guarded secrets, but the best suits of armor covered the entire body and allowed a knight to remain astonishingly nimble. The idea that a knight had to be winched up, hoisted, and lowered onto his horse is not true.

During the sixteenth century, the most expensive suits of armor copied the fashions of courtly clothing. German armor often looked as if it was made of pleated fabric, whereas Italian armor was generally smoother. Suits were painted black or were given a blue color during heating, while suits at the top end of the market were engraved with designs or even gilded with gold.

Going to War

In the early Middle Ages, monarchs relied on the feudal system when they wanted to raise an army. During times of peace, there was no need to have thousands of knights continually at the ready. In England, for example, when Henry II became king in 1154, the country emerged from a time of civil war. Many barons preferred to pay a tax called scutage (shield money) rather than provide the service of knights. Gradually, scutage became an annual tax, and Henry used the money to hire knights and soldiers when he needed them in France, where England owned large areas of land. These hired troops were called mercenaries.

King Edward I of England, who reigned from 1272 to 1307, fought a series of battles in Wales and Scotland. He needed troops for long periods of time and recruited them by means of what were called indentures. Once the king had agreed with a trusted nobleman how many troops he would provide and how much he would be paid, a clerk wrote out the details of the agreement twice, on a large piece of parchment. This was then cut into two pieces along a jagged line. The king kept one

The duke of Lancaster lays siege to Brest Castle, 1373, from a fifteenth-century manuscript illustration. Note, on the lower left, cannons and a primitive forge to repair weapons.

A fifteenth-century manuscript illustration showing French cavalry fighting English infantry during the Hundred Years' War. The English have lowered their lances as protection against a cavalry charge.

part of the parchment and the nobleman the other part. Both parties then had proof of their agreement, because the two pieces of parchment would fit together like teeth. The indenture derived its name from the French word *dent*, meaning "tooth."

Foot Soldiers

By the fourteenth century, knights in an army were greatly outnumbered by foot soldiers and archers. For example, Edward I used 25,000 men-at-arms, or infantry, but only

5,000 horsemen in his campaigns against the Welsh and Scots. These troops wore iron helmets and aketons, or leather jackets, sometimes riveted with metal plates.

The foot soldier in the later Middle Ages often carried a sword and a dagger, but it was a weapon variously known as a pike, poleaxe, or halberd that made him so effective. These weapons combined the features of both the spear and the axe, giving foot soldiers the potential to defeat mounted knights. Indeed, Flemish pikemen at the Battle of Courtrai in 1302 defeated an army of French knights, killing over 1,000 of them. This was the first occasion that foot soldiers had scored such a victory. Soldiers also started to make limited use of firearms during the late fourteenth century.

Archers

It was the archers that knights feared most. The Bayeux Tapestry shows Norman archers using fairly short bows at the Battle of Hastings, but by the thirteenth century, the longbow was changing the way in which battles were fought. Edward I was the first monarch to realize the potential of the longbow when he saw it being used by the Welsh. The arrow, fired from a six-foot bow made of elm, was capable of piercing an oak door four inches thick. When fired over a distance, it was accurate up to about 200 yards and could reach up to 400 yards.

It took great strength and skill to use the bow. Boys started to practice on smaller bows, and at one stage in England all male peasants were required by law to practice on their village green, shooting at targets called butts. An archer wore a bracer on the left wrist to provide support as he pulled the bowstring, and on the right hand he wore a glove to protect the fingers. Arrows between thirty and thirty-six inches long had a pointed steel tip capable of penetrating chain mail. At short range, one of these steel-tipped arrows could also penetrate plate armor. Goose feathers were used at the other end of the arrow to provide stability as it flew through the air.

The bow was strung before battle, and arrows were carried in a quiver worn on the hip. In battle, the arrows were usually stuck in the ground in front of the archer so they could be grabbed quickly. Standing in ranks, archers would fire wave after wave of arrows high in the air, causing injury and huge loss of life to enemy troops. Knights might be safe at a distance, but their horses would rear up and cause chaos when hit. If enemy knights charged, archers standing behind rows of sharpened stakes would wait until the knights were within range and then shoot with devastating accuracy.

The crossbow was very different in design and was favored by soldiers in most countries on mainland Europe. A much shorter and stiffer bow was mounted at the end of a wooden handle called a stock. The string on the bow was pulled back with a hook and held ready for firing by the nut, which was a notch in a revolving cylinder. A quarrel, or bolt, was then placed in a groove running along the length of the stock and was fired when the trigger released the nut. Crossbows could be used by relatively unskilled troops and were accurate and very powerful over quite a distance, though they lacked the range of the longbow. Later models used mechanical cranks to winch back the bowstring. The big disadvantage of the crossbow was the length of time it took to reload, whereas a skilled man with a longbow could shoot six or more arrows per minute.

King Edward III of England assaults the city of Caen in France in 1346, from a fourteenth-century French manuscript.

Before a Battle

There were literally hundreds of battles fought throughout Europe during the Middle Ages, so readiness was important. Fletchers were kept busy producing arrows, craftsmen made armor, and there was a constant need to breed suitable horses and keep them well shod. If it was going to be a long campaign, or if an army was expected to travel abroad, then many people in addition to knights and soldiers would be off to war.

The English army would commandeer merchant ships if crossing the channel to fight in France. When it arrived, the army would need to be fed. Soldiers raided farms and peasant homes, carrying off whatever food they could find. Horses also needed to graze, and if possible, military activity was planned for the summer months when the grass was tall.

Surprise was often crucial. Spies may have been reporting information about the enemy for weeks or even months, but as a battle approached, small detachments of horsemen were sent to carry out reconnaissance. They needed to track the enemy and also look for a suitable battleground, as geographical advantage could make all the difference. Positioning your forces on a hill meant the enemy would have to attack by charging up a slope, or perhaps a wooded area might hide troops until they were required.

Opposing armies might camp quite close to each other for several days before a battle. At night, nobles and knights slept in tents while foot soldiers huddled around hundreds of campfires. During the day, soldiers might be ordered to cut down trees to prepare defensive stakes. Devices known as caltrops were spread over the ground on which the enemy would charge. These were made of metal and had four sharp prongs sticking out in different directions. When thrown down, they always landed with one prong pointing upward, causing injury if trodden on by a man or horse.

Nobles met to discuss their battle plans, and at some point a commander might send his herald to the enemy camp to offer peace terms. If one side greatly outnumbered the other, then perhaps the smaller army might be persuaded to turn back. However, a smaller force might have no other option than to

In this fifteenth-century Italian manuscript illustration, an army besieges a castle. On the left a soldier can be seen preparing a ballista, a catapult for hurling stones.

fight. If there was time before a battle, a priest said prayers and troops would cross them-selves. Then the king or commanding noble might give a rousing speech to encourage everyone on to victory.

During a Battle

Battles were noisy affairs with clashing weapons, shouting, and screaming. Troop maneuvers would be signaled by trumpets, and drumbeats accompanied the foot soldiers as they marched forward.

Tactics were often influenced by tradition, and there was almost a set order of battle suggesting when archers should fire and when knights were to charge. It is said that some commanders consulted manuals dating back to Roman times. Tradition also dictated that men of the same rank should fight each other, so knights would engage in individual combat while ranks of foot soldiers attacked each other. Sometimes these conventions were ignored. Henry V of England caused outrage during the Battle of Agincourt in

A fifteenth-century illustration of knights in combat reveals something of the chaos of battle. Foot soldiers attack each other with swords and daggers. Mounted knights unhorse each other with lances.

1415 when he gave his foot soldiers the signal to hack to death hundreds of knights stuck in the mud.

Defending the standard, or flag, was regarded as important, as it was a rallying point for troops. To lose a flag was a disgrace and would indicate that the enemy was winning. During the Crusades, Sir Richard de Guise lost his left hand but fought on, holding his standard with a bloody stump. Beside him, the earl of Salisbury, William Longespée, lost a foot and both arms as he continued to defend the standard. They were both killed, having refused protection if they surrendered.

After a Battle

Victorious foot soldiers swiftly killed enemy troops lying injured and dying. Their own injured would be carried off using shields as stretchers. Heralds compiled lists of the dead, and soldiers stripped bodies of their weapons and armor and then pillaged local villages and towns. A knight who had been captured alive was held for ransom and spent months or even years in an enemy castle until his family paid for his release. Knights held as prisoners were usually treated with civility. During the twelfth century in France, a religious group called the Trinitarians was formed specifically to help negotiate the release of knights. In 1250, the French king was held ransom by Saracens during the Crusades. He was later released, after having surrendered the Egyptian city of Damietta and handing over a vast quantity of gold.

The Battle of Hastings, 1066, as depicted in the famous Bayeux Tapestry. An important technical innovation, shown here, was the stirrup, which freed the arms of the Norman horsemen to wield their weapons more effectively.

Famous Wars and Battles

 he following descriptions of some famous battles show the variety of ways in which medieval battles were fought and why these battles were won or lost.

The Battle of Hastings, October 14, 1066

The Battle of Hastings is important for several reasons. First, we know a good deal about it because there is documentation in the Bayeux Tapestry and in the *Anglo-Saxon Chronicle*. Second, the battle is of interest because the Saxons in England and the Normans from France fought using different weapons and battle tactics. Third, the Norman victory led to changes in the way England was governed, and for a number of centuries, linked the histories of England and France closely together, which in turn led to further war.

Edward the Confessor, the Saxon king of England, died in 1066. He left no heir, and so England's most powerful noble, Harold Godwinson, was crowned. However, across the channel Duke William of Normandy claimed that both Edward and Harold had promised him the throne. He immediately prepared an army and a large fleet.

The king of Norway also claimed the throne and landed in northern England during the summer of 1066. Harold defeated him at Stamford Bridge, near York, before hearing that William had arrived on the south coast. Tired but determined, Harold marched his army south again.

The Bayeux Tapestry shows that the Normans were well organized. They brought with them everything they needed, including horses for their knights and even a prefabricated wooden fort. Having landed, they set about gathering food, but William knew he had to win a decisive battle soon, so he set about burning local villages, hoping that Harold would hurry all the faster to defend his kingdom.

The Saxons took up a good defensive position behind a shield wall on Senlac Hill, near Hastings. Their most experienced troops were the housecarls, armed with huge double-headed axes. They fought with great heroism, as if rooted to the ground. In contrast, the more sophisticated style of warfare used by the Normans demanded organized battle tactics and the controlled use of troops.

At first, the Normans at the foot of the hill tried to break up the Saxon ranks by using archers. Then their knights, armed with spears, charged, although the effort of climbing the hill must have been considerable. For several hours, the Saxons withstood the showers of arrows and the charge of the knights, but then came the turning point in the battle. Some less experienced Saxon soldiers thought they saw Norman knights in retreat and left their hilltop position to give chase. Was this a Norman trick? Disorganized and on foot, the Saxons were easily killed by the Norman knights and soldiers waiting at the bottom of the hill.

The Battle of Crecy, 1346, like Agincourt a half century later, was another English victory over the French brought about by English archers with Welsh longbows.

The tide of the battle turned further when Harold was killed. The Bayeux Tapestry shows that he was struck in the eye by an arrow and then hacked down by knights. His mutilated body was later placed under a pile of stones on the cliffs near Hastings, and only after many years was he given a proper burial at Waltham Abbey, north of London. William meanwhile marched to London, where he was crowned on the twenty-fifth of December.

Courtrai, "The Battle of the Gold Spurs," July 11, 1302

For much of the Middle Ages, a charge by knights on horseback was decisive in many battles. In Italy, for example, knights reigned supreme. However, the Battle of Courtrai showed that organized foot soldiers were capable of defeating such an enemy.

Philip IV of France incorporated Flanders into his kingdom in 1300. This was a wealthy land covering roughly the same area as modern-day Belgium. The occupation and the unfair taxes that Philip imposed encouraged the people of Flanders to rise in rebellion. In 1302, the people of Bruges killed a number of French knights, and Philip decided to send an army to stamp out further rebellion.

On July 8, the French, led by Robert Artois, arrived at the Flemish town of Courtrai. Their army numbered 6,500 and included 2,500 knights. The Flemish army opposing them numbered 9,000 but consisted of only foot soldiers. Apart from about 400 nobles, they were mostly untrained craftsmen and peasants, led by Pieter de Coninck.

The French held a council of war. Although outnumbered, they decided to teach their enemy a lesson with a full frontal charge. The Flemish troops expected this and so they positioned themselves behind two brooks and an area of marshy ground, which some reports say they disguised with brushwood. In their arrogance, the French forgot to carry out the usual reconnaissance. Many of the knights managed to jump their horses successfully across the brooks, whereupon they became stuck in the boggy ground beyond. The Flemish troops had been told not to take any prisoners and so they slaughtered the stranded knights with pikes.

After the battle, 500 gold spurs were stripped from the French knights and taken to the Church of Our Lady in Courtrai. There they adorned a vault until the French reclaimed them when they defeated a Flemish army in 1382. The Battle of Courtrai was significant because the people of Flanders regained their independence. They also inspired other ordinary foot soldiers to take on massed ranks of knights. The Scots, for example, were standing behind a burn, or brook, when they defeated English knights at the Battle of Bannockburn in 1314.

Sluys, June 24, 1340

The famous sea battle fought at Sluys came at the beginning of a long series of battles fought between England and France from 1337 to 1453, which later came to be known as the Hundred Years' War. Since the Battle of Hastings in 1066, English monarchs had ruled vast amounts of land in France, and the Hundred Years' War was really a struggle between the two countries over which areas they would each control. The wine-growing area of Bordeaux, for example, was especially valued for the trade it produced, and the city of Bordeaux itself was held by the English until 1453.

On June 24, 1340, Edward III of England set off toward Flanders (the home country of his wife) with a large army carried by a fleet of about 200 ships. As he approached the port of Sluys, a French fleet was seen, drawn up in defensive formation, with ships tied together in several lines. Their

The naval battle at Sluys, off the coast of Flanders, 1340. Before the age of the cannon, ships simply grappled with each other, and their soldiers fought across the decks as if it was a battle on land.

aim was to prevent the English from landing. Edward ordered his fleet to maneuver so that the wind and the sun were behind them.

The English ships had wooden battlements, or towers, at the front of each vessel, called the bow. As the English fleet came within range, archers equipped with longbows fired from these forecastles, as they were called, killing hundreds of French soldiers and sailors and giving the English the upper hand early in the battle. When the enemy ships came alongside each other, grappling irons were thrown, pulling the ships tightly together. Furious hand-to-hand

The Battle of Agincourt, 1415, from a fifteenth-century illuminated manuscript. Though the artist has depicted both armies protected by archers, the French mounted knights recklessly charged—and were slaughtered by—the English archers.

fighting took place on the decks, while high up in crows' nests, soldiers hurled down huge stones, attempting to sink enemy ships.

This was certainly one of the bloodiest battles of the Middle Ages, partly because at sea there was no hope of escape. In addition to losing a large number of ships, about 18,000 French soldiers were killed, while English losses were relatively few. From then on, raids across the channel were unhindered, and English bowmen continued to be crucial during the Hundred Years' War, winning further victories at Crécy in 1346 and Poitiers in 1356. Perhaps the most famous victory won by archers was at Agincourt in 1415, when the French lost thousands of men and the English only a few hundred.

The Battle of Bosworth, August 22, 1485

The Battle of Bosworth concluded the Wars of the Roses—the thirty-year struggle between the nobles of the houses of York and Lancaster for control of the English throne—and brought the Middle Ages to a close in England. What is of particular interest is that until very late in the battle either side could have won. The balance was held by 6,000 soldiers who waited on one side of the field as their commander, Lord Stanley, made up his mind which side to support.

King Richard III was a controversial figure who commanded loyalty from many but was hated by others. He grabbed the English crown by allegedly murdering his two young nephews, both of whom were before him in line of succession to the throne. Eventually, Richard was challenged by Henry Tudor, who also claimed the crown. Henry had been in exile in France, but when he landed in Wales with just 2,000 men, he marched east, gathering more troops as he went.

The two sides met at Bosworth, near Leicester. Richard arrived first and arranged his troops on Ambion Hill. He was supported by the duke of Norfolk, while Henry was supported by the earl of Oxford. Richard also expected Lord Stanley to support him, but the situation was delicate because Stanley was Henry Tudor's stepfather. As a precaution, Richard took Stanley's own son, Lord Strange, as a hostage. If Stanley did not support Richard, his son would be executed. But Lord Stanley saw that if he supported Richard, and Henry were to win, he would be out of favor with the new king. He therefore waited to see how the battle developed.

Suspecting Stanley's treachery, Richard led a group of knights in a brave charge straight at Henry. If Richard could kill his enemy, the battle would be over. It was now that Stanley ordered his troops into battle, to make sure of Henry's victory. Richard immediately ordered Lord Strange's execution, but his guards decided to release him, seeing that this would put them in a better position if Henry won the battle. Richard was the last English king to die in battle. He was taken off to be buried at Leicester, slumped naked over the back of a horse. Meanwhile, on the battlefield, Lord Stanley crowned his stepson, who became Henry VII.

Castles at War

astles played a crucial role in the warfare of the Middle Ages. Along with cathedrals, they were the largest and most impressive buildings to appear in Europe since the days of the Romans. Castles were obviously designed to provide safety and maximum defense for the people who lived in them. However, they also provided a base from which attacks might be launched if an enemy army invaded.

Defense of a Castle

The earliest castles during the Middle Ages were of motte and bailey construction. A mound of earth was made, on which was built a small wooden tower, or keep, which was protected by a wall of wooden stakes. Around the motte was another wall of stakes enclosing an area in which there were living quarters and storerooms. A ditch surrounded the whole site.

Motte and bailey castles were gradually replaced by stronger stone castles, which were less vulnerable to fire. The enormous weight of the stone keeps meant that they could not be built on an artificial mound, so castles were

A fifteenth-century manuscript illustration depicting the French army laying siege to a fortified town. Note the use of crossbows and cannons. In the distance, ships at sea complete the blockade.

often built on natural rocky hills. Where this was not possible, extra protection might be given by diverting a river to create a moat filled with water around the castle.

The square corners of stone keeps could be badly damaged by rocks hurled by catapults and siege machines, so round keeps and outer curtain walls started to appear by the mid-thirteenth century. Missiles glanced off their smooth surfaces. Later still, rings of two or even three concentric outer walls were built.

Castles became more and more ingenious in their design. The entrance was always a weak spot and so would be protected by a drawbridge. A sliding iron gate called a portcullis could be lowered over the entrance itself. Then there would often be a short tunnel before another portcullis. Any attackers trapped in the tunnel would have boiling pitch or water poured on them through holes in the roof. Another protection for the entrance was the barbican, a kind of three-sided tower raised over an open alleyway.

The tops of walls were given crenellations or parapets from behind which arrows could be fired. Ledges were built jutting out from the battlements for defenders to drop rocks or fend off siege ladders. The bases of castle walls sloped outward, so rocks dropped from above bounced off horizontally toward the enemy. Windows were narrow slits when viewed from outside, but inside they widened sharply to allow archers to fire in all directions. If attackers did manage to breach the entrance to a castle, they would have little hope of going any farther. Even spiral stairs were designed so that only a soldier coming down or retreating in defense could swing a sword.

At the first sign of danger, extra supplies would be brought within castle walls, including local farm animals. Any crops not harvested might be burned to prevent them being used by enemy troops. When an army arrived to besiege a castle, heralds would meet to negotiate. If the inhabitants did not agree to surrender at this stage, they could expect no mercy later if the castle was captured. A siege could last for many months or even years. Defenders were left hoping that a relief army would arrive, but meanwhile felt cut off from the outside world. During the Crusades, Turks used carrier pigeons to send and receive messages when besieged. In

A castle surrenders, from a fifteenth-century manuscript illustration. The soldiers of the besieging army are marching through the gate into the castle.

response, the European soldiers used birds of prey trained to kill other birds. Conditions in the castle would meanwhile decline rapidly. The spread of illness and disease was a constant fear, water supplies ran low, and when food was short the occupants would search for rats to eat.

Attacking a Castle

As the defense of castles became more effective, the methods of attack became increasingly more ingenious. Starving a castle into surrender might take a very long time, but at least it was relatively safe. On the other hand, attacking a castle directly was very dangerous. Any town near a castle would probably fall quite quickly. Burning arrows would set fire to thatched houses, while troops used battering rams on gates and scaled walls on long ladders. Much larger siege machines were needed to breach castle walls.

A besieging army might arrive with giant crossbows and catapults in pieces, which would be reconstructed on site. Ballistas were used to fire large metal bolts, and mangonels threw boulders from an arm shaped like a large spoon. Ropes at one end of the arm were twisted to provide tension, while the other end was held fast and loaded just before release. Both of these weapons dated back to Roman times and were of limited effectiveness.

More terrifying was the trebuchet. This was a truly enormous catapult, capable of hurling stones weighing between 100 and 200 pounds over several hundred yards. At one end of a long arm was a large container filled with rocks that acted as a counterbalance. At the other end of the arm was a sling, which whipped around in the air to give extra propulsion to

In 1450, the French besieged the town of Cherbourg, which had been captured by the English. Archers and cannons are evident.

the missile before its release. King Edward I of England ordered a trebuchet to be built during his campaign against Scotland. It was called Warwolf, and with an arm about fifty feet long, it threw boulders with such force that they penetrated castle walls.

Catapults were also used to throw diseased animal carcasses into castles in an effort to spread disease. Between 1097 and 1098 it took a crusading army eight months to capture the Turkish-held city of Antioch (now Antakya). During the siege, 200 decapitated Turkish heads were catapulted into the castle in an attempt to demoralize the defenders. Eventually, an armorer turned traitor and opened the gates. Elsewhere, there were stories

A modern artist's depiction of the French attack on Dover Castle in 1216. One of the towers protecting the gate has collapsed, and on the right, archers on a siege tower seek protection behind a wicker wall.

that enemy heralds were put into catapults and sent flying back into the castle grounds!

Another technique used to gain entry to a castle involved filling the moat with earth and stones to allow a siege tower to be pushed up against a castle wall. The siege tower was a tall wooden construction on wheels, covered on the outside by animal hides that were soaked in water to prevent the tower from being set on fire. Soldiers climbed up ladders inside the tower and then over a drawbridge and onto the castle battlements. A huge, metal, pointed battering ram, suspended under a roof, could also be pushed on wheels up to a gate. Rocks thrown from above made this a hazardous operation, but archers standing behind wicker fences tried to shoot defenders on the castle walls.

Perhaps the most time-consuming way to break into a castle involved mining underneath the castle walls by digging a tunnel supported by wood posts. When the tunnel was completed, it was filled with branches and then set on fire. The aim was to bring down the castle wall as the posts shoring up the tunnel collapsed.

Cannons and Guns

Gunpowder, a mixture of saltpeter, sulfur, and charcoal, was probably discovered first in China. Knowledge of its use spread west to the Arab world and then to Europe, where the earliest illustration of a cannon, called a bombard, dates from 1327. The first cannons were made from strips of metal bound together by hoops, making them quite dangerous to use. As late as 1460, King James II of Scotland was killed while standing too close to a cannon that exploded. Later cannons were made of cast metal. Their range was further improved by the development of better gunpowder in granule form, and safer ways of firing cannons were also devised.

At first, cannons were used in sieges rather like catapults, merely to fire rocks. Soon metal balls were found to be more effective, and cannons were able to end a siege in a matter of weeks. In the mid-fifteenth century, thanks to the increasing effectiveness of cannons, the French drove the English from France as they quickly recaptured English-held castles. At about the same time, the kings of northern Spain drove the Moors from their castles in southern Spain.

Castles themselves were now being redesigned to cope with this new threat. Battlements were being strengthened, and castles were also mounting cannons on their walls. As early as 1381, Bologna in Italy had thirty-five cannons. It was difficult to use cannons in open battle, partly because they were so heavy to transport. Nevertheless, they certainly caused fear. Early muskets were also of limited use in battle because they were difficult to hold when fired. They operated like miniature cannons and had special hooks to fit over walls to cope with

The siege of Montaigne, 1360, by the army of Edward the Black Prince. On the left, a siege tower protecting the attacking archers also contains some primitive cannons. More soldiers are arriving by sea.

the recoil when fired. They gradually improved and became more effective, but at first they were best used in siege warfare.

The increasing use of cannons and firearms changed the pattern of warfare and helped to bring the Middle Ages to a close. Once masses of common infantrymen possessed firearms that could penetrate armor and bring down mounted horsemen at a distance of several hundred yards, the whole reason for the existence of a privileged caste of warrior knights disappeared, and along with them their code of valor and individual combat. The change began with the appearance of the Welsh longbow, and by the time reliable firearms were introduced, the glory was disappearing from the battlefield.

Glossary

aketon   Padded jacket worn by knights under chain mail to help soften sword blows. Also worn by foot soldiers.

axe   A weapon with a flat metal cutting edge at the end of a wooden shaft, swung by one or two hands.

ball and chain   A metal ball covered in spikes and attached by a short chain to a wooden shaft.

ballista   Giant crossbow, used for firing large metal arrows during sieges.

barbican   Protected approach to a city or castle gate, consisting of an open alley surrounded by a three-sided tower.

baron   High-ranking noble.

bascinet   Close-fitting helmet with round surfaces to deflect sword blows.

battering ram   Tree trunk or beam with a metal-tipped end, used for battering down castle and city gates.

battlements   Raised parapets at the tops of walls, which gave protection against enemy arrows.

bawdrick   Waist belt from which a sword was hung.

Bayeux Tapestry   A long tapestry that depicts the events of 1066 leading up to and including the Battle of Hastings.

bombard   Early type of cannon.

butt   Round target for archery practice.

byrnie   Chain mail shirt, also called a hauberk.

caltrop   Piece of twisted iron with four small, sharp prongs, thrown down on the ground before battles to cause injury to men and horses.

chain mail   Flexible armor made of interlocking rings of iron.

chivalry   Code of behavior for knights during times of war and peace.

coat of arms   Emblem or badge on a shield, surcoat, or flag indicating family background.

concentric walls   Rings of defensive walls around a castle.

crenellations   Defensive battlements on a castle wall, used to provide shelter for protection, with openings for firing arrows.

crossbow   Bow set at right angles to a wooden handle, used for firing metal-tipped bolts called quarrels.

Crusades   Wars fought by European soldiers against Muslims who had captured Jerusalem and the Holy Land.

cuir bouilli   Type of protective armor made of stiff, boiled leather.

curtain wall   Outer wall of a castle.

drawbridge   Bridge that could be lowered over a moat or ditch.

duke   Very high-ranking nobleman, related to the king or queen.

fletcher   Person who makes arrows.

forecastle   A raised wooden tower at the front of a ship.

gauntlet   Protective glove made of armor.

halberd   Long pole with a metal spear and axe at one end.

hauberk   Chain-mail shirt.

herald   High-ranking servant who acted as a messenger and who also organized tournaments.

joust   Competition during which knights charged at each other on horseback with blunt lances.

jupon   A short surcoat.

keep   Main building at the center of a castle.

longbow   Bow made of elm, about six feet long, capable of shooting arrows with great power and accuracy.

mangonel   Type of catapult used when laying siege to a castle.

mêlée   Mock free-for-all battle at a tournament.

mercenary   Soldier hired to fight and often originating from another country.

misericord   Dagger used to kill wounded knights.

moat   Ditch, filled with water, surrounding a castle.

Moors   Muslims from North Africa.

motte and bailey   Early style of castle, with a keep on an earthen mound, surrounded by an enclosed area, constructed of wood.

page   Boy undertaking the first steps of training to become a knight.

pike   Long pole with a metal spear and axe or hook at one end.

pillage   The act of raiding houses after battle to steal valuables.

quarrel   Bolt fired by a crossbow.

quintain   Revolving target used to practice jousting skills.

quiver   Holder for arrows, worn over the shoulder or on
  a belt.

sabaton   Armor protection for the feet.

scutage   Tax paid to the king instead of providing troops
  for battle.

stirrup   Metal rest or support for the feet while on horseback.

surcoat   Cloth coat-of-arms worn over chain mail.

trebuchet   Siege machine with a long arm that threw
  large rocks.

visor   Removable front of a knight's helmet.

For More Information

The Columbia University Medieval Guild
602 Philosophy Hall, Columbia University
New York, NY 10027
e-mail: cal36@columbia.edu
Web site: http://www.cc.columbia.edu/cu/medieval

The Dante Society of America
Brandeis University, MS 024
P.O. Box 549110
Waltham, MA 02454-9110
e-mail: dsa@dantesociety.org
Web site: http://www.dantesociety.org

International Courtly Literature Society
North American Branch
c/o Ms. Sara Sturm-Maddox
Department of French and Italian
University of Massachusetts at Amherst
Amherst, MA 01003
e-mail: ssmaddox@frital.umass.edu
Web site: http://www-dept.usm.edu/~engdept/icls/
      iclsnab.htm

Medieval Academy of America
1430 Massachusetts Avenue
Cambridge, MA 02138
(617) 491-1622
e-mail: Speculum@medievalacademy.org
Web site: http://www.medievalacademy.org/t_bar_2.htm

Rocky Mountain Medieval and Renaissance Association
Department of English Language and Literature
University of Northern Iowa
Cedar Falls, IA 50614-0502
(319) 273-2089
e-mail: jesse.swan@uni.edu
Web site: http://www.uni.edu/~swan/rmmra/rocky.htm

Web Sites

Due to the changing nature of Internet links, the Rosen Publishing Group, Inc., has developed an online list of Web sites related to the subject of this book. This site is updated regularly. Please use this link to access the list:

http://www.rosenlinks.com/lma/wewa

For Further Reading

Bartlett, Clive. *English Longbowmen 1330–1515.* Oxford: Osprey Publishing, 2002.

Cootes, Richard John. *The Middle Ages.* New York: Longman, 1996.

Gravett, Christopher. *Castle.* London: Dorling Kindersley, 1994.

Gravett, Christopher. *Knight.* London: Dorling Kindersley, 1993.

Gravett, Christopher. *Knights at Tournament.* Oxford: Osprey Publishing, 1988.

Hook, Richard, and Christa Hook. *Medieval Siege Warfare.* Oxford: Osprey Publishing, 1990.

Kelly, Nigel, Rosemary Rees, and Jane Shuter. *Medieval Realms.* Oxford: Heinemann, 1997.

Langley, Andrew. *Castle at War.* London: Dorling Kindersley, 1998.

Steele, Philip. *The Medieval World.* London: Kingfisher, 2000.

Bibliography

Gravett, Christopher. *Knights at Tournament.* Oxford: Osprey Publishing, 1988.

Guest, Ken, and Denise Guest. *British Battles.* London: HarperCollins, 1997.

Hogg, Ian V. *The Encyclopedia of Weaponry.* London: Greenwich Editions, 1998.

Hook, Richard, and Christa Hook. *Medieval Siege Warfare.* Oxford: Osprey Publishing, 1990.

Jones, John. *The Medieval World.* Walton on Thames, England: Thomas Nelson Ltd., 1979.

Matthew, Donald. *Atlas of Medieval Europe.* Oxford: Phaidon Press Ltd., 1983.

Norman, Vesey. *Arms and Armour.* London: Octopus Books, 1972.

Parker, Geoffrey. *Warfare.* Cambridge, England: Cambridge University Press, 2000.

Rothero, Christopher. *Medieval Military Dress.* Poole, England: Blandford Press, 1983.

Seymour, William. *Battles in Britain.* London: Book Club Associates, 1979.

Wilkinson, Frederick. *Arms and Armour.* London: Chancellor Press, 1978.

Index

About the Author

Paul Hilliam is a graduate of London University. He is senior master at Derby Grammar School in England where he has enjoyed teaching history and religious studies. He has traveled throughout Europe, the Middle East, and India, visiting sites of historical interest.

Photo Credits

Cover, pp. 6, 45, 52 © British Library/Art Archive;pp. 4 © Bibliothèque Nationale Paris/Art Archive; p. 7 © Dagli Orti/ Biblioteca Nazionale Turin/Art Archive; p. 9 © Dagli Orti/Bibliotheque Nationale Paris/Art Archive; p. 11 © Dagli Orti/Biblioteca Nazionale Marciana Venice/Art Archive; pp. 13, 26, 40 © HarperCollins Publishers/Bibliothéque Nationale Paris/Art Archive; p. 14 © Erich Lessing/AKG London; p. 16 © Joseph Martin/Album/ Art Archive; p. 18 © AKG London; p. 20 © Royal Armouries; p. 21 © Dagli Orti/Biblioteca Estense Modena/Art Archive; p. 25 © JFB/Art Archive; p. 29 © Dagli Orti/Musées de la Tapisserie Bayeux/ Art Archive; p. 31 © The Bodleian Library Oxford/Art Archive; p. 32 © Dagli Orti/Musée Condé Chantilly; p. 34 © Dagli Orti/Musée de la Tapisseries Bayeux/Art Archive; pp. 37, 41, 49 © Bibliothéque Nationale Paris/Art Archive; p. 47 © Dagli Orti/Bibliothéque Municipale Reims/Art Archive; p. 50 © Mike Seaforth/English Heritage.

Designer: Geri Fletcher; **Editor:** Jake Goldberg; **Photo Researcher:** Elizabeth Loving